THIS POETRY CONTAINS SARCASM

things i can't say

DINA
EZZEDDINE

copyrights
go here

i didn't care enough to add this. but have too!

i don't care, these
poems are stupid.

-SARCASM IN POETRY

table
of contents

there was supposed to be a table of contents here...

... i removed it to piss you off!

THIS POEM IS STUPID

Oh what a masterpiece, this poem divine
Filled with such sarcasm, so cleverly designed
I don't care for its brilliance, it's simply sublime
Truly, it sucks, but hey, that's just fine

Each word dripping with irony, so sharp and clear
Leaving me in awe, with a sarcastic sneer
Who needs beauty or grace, when we have disdain
This poem's sarcasm, is truly insane

So keep up the mockery, the wit, the jest
For this poem may suck, but it's still the best
In its own snarky way, it shines like a star
So cheers to sarcasm, no matter how bizarre.

OKAY SO WHAT?

Oh, what a masterpiece, this poem is so dumb
A true epic tale, a work of art for the numb
With each line so profound, it's hard to understand
The depth of stupidity, in this poet's hand

A journey of nonsense, a quest for the witless
Oh, what a delight, this foolishness is endless
With every word uttered, a cringe-worthy sight
This epic poem so dull, it puts the stars alight

So let us raise a toast, to this poem so absurd
A true masterpiece of idiocy, we must be assured
For in the annals of time, it shall be revered
As the greatest display of foolishness, ever
endeared.

JUST GO AWAY....

Oh, so now what? I don't care,
The epic tale of my life is a flair.
Sarcasm dripping from my tongue,
In a world where folly is flung.

I mock the trials that come my way,
For I am the hero of this play.
No challenge too great, no foe too tough,
I overcome, I strut and I strut.

So now what, you ask with a sneer?
I'll keep on shining, have no fear.
For in this epic saga of mine,
I'll scoff at fate and continue to shine.

FOR THE LOVE OF GOD

Oh my god, for the love of god,
Why must poetry be so flawed?
With its flowery words and lofty themes,
It's like a nightmare from which I can't wake.
Epic tales of love and war,
But really, who even cares anymore?
I'd rather watch paint dry or grass grow,
Than listen to this pretentious show.
So let's raise a toast to dumb poetry,
For making us all dumber, you see.

SUCK IT UP

Behold, the epic tale of woe,
For those who despise my sarcasm flow.
I'll twist and turn my words with glee,
Just to spite those who can't see.

You say sarcasm has no place,
In poetry's noble embrace.
But I'll continue to crack wise,
For your narrow mind, I despise.

So suck it up, my dear friend,
For sarcasm has no end.
In this epic of words so sly,
I'll leave you rolling your eyes, oh my!

DO THESE POEMS OFFEND YOU?

In the world of poetry, I reign supreme,
With words so potent, they might make you scream.
But did I offend you with my verse?
Oh, how tragic, I thought it was a gift, not a curse.

My lines cut deeper than a sword,
So delicate souls may find them absurd.
But fear not, for my epic rhyme,
Will stand the test of space and time.

So if my poetry has struck a nerve,
Just remember, it's not for the weak to observe.
For in this poetic realm, I am king,
And my words are sharper than any sting.

HEY DIMWIT, DOES THIS OFFEND YOU?

In a world where logic reigns supreme,
I must ask, are you living in a dream?
Do you wander through life without a clue,
Or are you just naturally dimwitted, it's true?

Are you stupid or just born that way,
To lack intelligence day by day?
Do you make decisions without a thought,
Or are you simply lacking what you were taught?

I wonder as I watch you stumble and fall,
If there's any sense in you at all.
Perhaps it's not your fault, you see,
Maybe you were just meant to be.

So carry on in your foolish way,
I'll watch from afar, amused by your display.
For in a world so full of wit and wonder,
You stand out as a comical blunder.

Do my poems offend you?

.... good! that was my intension.

WHY IS YOUR FACE LIKE THAT?

Oh, is your face seriously like that,
Or are you just dumb as a bat?
With your vacant stare and vacant smile,
I can't help but think, oh what a trial.

You must be joking, surely you jest,
To think that face is truly the best.
For with each glance, my eyes do burn,
At the sight of your face, I feel concern.

But alas, I must endure your gaze,
For it seems forever it will stay.
So I'll just smile and nod along,
But in my heart, I sing this song.

Oh, is your face seriously like that,
Or are you just dumb as a bat?
No matter the truth, I'll keep my cool,
For sarcasm is my golden rule.

I WRITE IN PENT UP RAGE

Oh how I love poetry, it fills me with such glee
The flow of words, the depth of thoughts, it really
speaks to me
But sometimes it irks me, it puts me in a rage
That's why I like to write with sarcasm, to vent my pent
up stage

Oh the beauty of language, the power it holds
But it also infuriates me, it's like my patience unfolds
I try to find solace in the verses that I pen
But sometimes the sweetness of poetry just isn't enough
for this hen

So I sprinkle in sarcasm, a little touch of snark
To let out all the frustration, to let out all the bark
Because sometimes poetry, it just ain't all that great
And that's why I write with sarcasm, to alleviate the
weight

So let the words flow freely, let the sarcasm reign
Because sometimes poetry, it just brings me pain
But with a little touch of snark, a little hint of sass
I can let out all the anger, and let out all the gas!

WRITING FRUSTRATES ME

In the world of poetry I dwell,
Where writing brings me endless hell,
Each word a struggle, each line a fight,
But sarcasm is my saving light.

I weave my words with twisted glee,
Mocking those who cannot see,
The humor in my twisted verse,
For writing is a dreadful curse.

So let the poets sing their praise,
While I scoff at their flowery ways,
For in this land of rhymes and stanzas,
Sarcasm is my grand extravaganza.

Writing frustrates me, this much is true,
But oh, the joy in mocking you,
In every line, in every verse,
Sarcasm is my sacred curse.

I DON'T WANT TO WRITE POEMS

Oh poetry, a cruel and endless hell,
Where my words twist and turn, never to excel,
Each line falls flat, a dismal show,
My verses stumble, my flow too slow.

I reach for the stars, but always fall short,
My rhymes feel forced, my metaphors distort,
Each stanza a struggle, a torturous plight,
Poetry mocking me, in the dead of night.

But still I write, despite the pain,
Hoping one day my words will reign,
For even in this hellish verse,
I find a spark, a blessing to nurse.

OOPS SORRY, DID I OFFEND YOU AGAIN?

In a world where words cut deep
I speak my mind, I will not keep
If you don't like what I say, tough luck
I won't change, I won't give a shrug

I'm made this way, this is who I am
I won't conform, I won't give a damn
So suck it up, deal with it
My words are sharp, my wit is lit

I won't soften my tongue for you
I'll say what I mean, always true
So if you can't handle the heat
Stay out of my way, take a seat

I'm not here to please or obey
I'll speak my mind, come what may
So if you don't like what I say
Suck it up, I'm made this way.

NOTHING IN THIS BOOK WORKS

Oh, dear, what's that you just said,
That my mind must be so dull and dead?
Well, bravo for your sharp wit and grace,
Your insults are a real disgrace.

Do tell me more of my foolish ways,
You must have seen through my clever ruse.
But wait, let me guess, you're just so clever,
Your words are like a gentle feather.

I must applaud your astute observation,
You've really nailed my imperfection.
But don't you worry, I'll try to improve,
Perhaps one day I'll match your groovy groove.

So thank you kind sir or madam,
For pointing out my utter madam.
I'll strive to reach your lofty height,
And maybe one day, I'll see the light.

Where you expecting a real good poetry book?

Sorry, I'll try better next time!

no I won't.

I CAN'T FIGURE OUT WHAT TO WRITE

Oh, what were you expecting, a great poem, you say?
I'm afraid my sarcasm is on full display,
For I'm no Wordsworth or Shakespeare, you see,
Just a jester of words, filled with irony.

You came looking for beauty, for phrases sublime,
But all you'll find here are words out of line.
No sonnets or odes, just a ballad that bites,
Full of wit and humor, to challenge your sights.

So if you're seeking perfection, pure poetry gold,
I'm afraid in that regard, I must leave you cold.
But if a touch of sarcasm is what you desire,
Then my friend, you're in luck, for that I do not tire.

So here's my creation, lacking in grace,
A poem of sarcasm, in your puzzled face.
I hope you're amused, or at least slightly irate,
For in this world of verse, irony is my fate.

THINGS YOU DON'T SAY TO YOUR BOSS

In the office, I must tread with care
For my boss's feelings I can't dare
To offend with my sharp wit and sass
So I hold back and bite my tongue like brass

I've got so much I want to say
But it would surely ruin my day
If I let loose with my sarcasm
And caused a major cataclysm

My friends too, they don't understand
The jokes I make, they're not so bland
But if I let my true self out
I fear they'll scream and shout

So here I am, smiling wide
And silently screaming inside
My words locked up, never to be free
For fear of offending thee.

I WANTED TO SAY THIS

I hope I offended you today, oh what a delightful
sensation
It was my intention, you see, to cause a bit of agitation
I chose my words carefully, with a touch of sarcasm
To leave you feeling irked, like a buzzing spasm

I relish in the thought of getting under your skin
To see you squirm and fume, makes my heart grin
I hope my words have struck a nerve, brought you some
dismay
For my goal was to offend you, in a playful way

So if you find yourself upset, angered or in pain
Just remember, dear friend, it was all done in vain
For I thrive on the drama, the chaos and strife
I hope I offended you today, it's just a part of life

PROMISE I WON'T SAY THIS TO YOU

Oh, the things you shouldn't say,
But my sarcasm gets in the way,
I'll give you a piece of my mind,
And leave your ego far behind.

I'll tell you how smart you are,
Even though you're a shooting star,
I'll praise your endless wit,
While silently thinking, "yeah, right, you twit."

I'll nod along to your every word,
While inside my thoughts are absurd,
I'll smile and laugh at your joke,
But inside I'm ready to choke.

So let's keep up this charade,
Where my sarcasm never fades,
I'll bite my tongue and play nice,
But trust me, I'm rolling the dice.

BUT I'LL SAY THIS INSTEAD

Oh, I promise not to use sarcasm today,
But you just had to push me all the way.
You've really outdone yourself this time,
So I'll say this with a pleasant chime.

Your actions are just so charming,
I really find them disarming.
You've got a real knack for getting on my nerves,
But hey, who am I to judge your little perversions.

I'll keep my words sweet and kind,
But deep down, I'm losing my mind.
So here's a little ballad just for you,
Hope you appreciate my sarcasm shining through.

FRIENDSHIP IS ABOUT THIS....

Oh wholly crap, you're such a fool,
Why am I friends with you, that's the golden rule.
Your stupidity knows no bound,
But somehow, our friendship is still around.

You never fail to amaze,
With your idiotic ways.
I must be a saint,
To put up with your brainless paint.

But I guess I need you,
To make me feel smart too.
So keep being dumb,
And I'll keep being glum.

Oh wholly crap, you're so absurd,
But hey, that's what friends are for, right? A nerd.

THINGS ~~NOT~~ TO SAY TO YOUR MOM

Oh, don't use sarcasm with your mom,
She'll think you're such a chum,
You'll see her eyes roll and hear her sigh,
As she wonders why oh why oh why.

She'll never appreciate your wit,
She'll just think you're being a little git,
So best to keep your mouth shut tight,
And avoid her disapproving sight.

For when you dare to be so sly,
She'll give you that dreaded mom eye,
And with a shake of her head,
You'll wish you were anywhere else instead.

So heed my warning, oh wayward child,
Don't risk mom's displeasure so wild,
For sarcasm with her just won't do,
She'll always see right through you.

Oh, your still here? Reading this are yeah!

Don't worry it sucks! This poetry is pure sarcasm.

... i won't be offended if you don't read on.

Maybe just a little offended!

TO MY LOVING BOYFRIEND

Oh boyfriend of mine, so kind and sweet,
I promise not to roll my eyes, oh what a feat,
I'll bite my tongue and hold back my thoughts,
Even though you clearly sold me short.

I won't say a word that might offend,
But oh, the sarcasm I'll pretend,
To be so understanding and patient with you,
Even though you've no clue what to do.

I'll smile and nod, and play along,
But deep down inside, you know I long,
To let my true feelings be known,
To show you how much I've grown.

So here's my promise, oh boyfriend of mine,
I'll keep my sarcasm under wraps, just this time,
But next time, watch out, for I'll let it all show,
I'll speak my mind, and let you know.

THIS IS ME TRYING

Oh, I promise with all my heart
To keep my sarcasm apart
I won't roll my eyes, oh no
And keep my mouth shut, don't you know?

I'll bite my tongue and hold it in
So you won't see my cheeky grin
I promise not to make you cry
With words that cut, oh me oh my

No more sly remarks from me
No more biting wit, you'll see
I'll be as sweet as sugar, dear
With no hint of sarcasm here

So rest assured, my friend so dear
I'll hold back the sarcasm, never fear
I promise to be oh so kind
With no sharp tongue, no mean mind

But deep down, we both know
That sarcasm's just a part of me, though
So forgive me if I slip
And let a sarcastic comment rip

But fear not, I'll try my best
To keep my sarcasm repressed
I promise, oh I do
Just don't hold me to it, will you?

BREATHING...

I'm trying so hard to hold it in,
My sarcasm, sharp as a pin.
I don't want to offend, oh no,
But the struggle is real, don't you know?

I'll bite my tongue and hold my breath,
To keep from delivering a sarcastic death.
I'll smile and nod, oh so sweet,
Even if my inner voice wants to speak.

So forgive me if I seem a bit fake,
I'm just trying to avoid a mistake.
I'll keep my sarcasm locked away,
For fear of upsetting you today.

DON'T CARE ...

Oh sorry, did I offend you today?
I was just hoping to ruin your day.
I hope you have a not so great time,
Filled with misery and sorrow, so sublime.

I'll sprinkle sarcasm in every word I say,
Just to make sure you have a terrible day.
I'll make sure everything goes wrong,
Just to make you feel like you don't belong.

So have a day full of despair,
With a touch of misery in the air.
I hope you regret crossing my path,
Because I'll make sure you feel my sarcastic wrath.

...STILL DON'T CARE

I don't care about your problems, oh no, not one bit
Keep babbling on, I just love hearing your wit
Your drama and your woes, they really make my day
I couldn't care less, so please don't stop, I pray

Your troubles and your woes, they captivate me so
I hang on every word, oh how I love your show
Your life is oh so interesting, I can't look away
But don't worry my friend, I still don't care, okay?

So keep on talking, keep on moaning and groaning
I'll sit here and listen, my interest never waning
Your problems are thrilling, truly top-notch
But honestly my dear, they don't even touch the spot

So go ahead, keep on whining and complaining
I'll just sit here, my boredom waning
Your drama is like music to my ears
But please do remember, I really don't care, my dear

PROBABLY NOT...

In a world filled with lies and deceit,
I find it hard to keep up with the beat.
Do I care about what you do?
Probably not, I've got better things in view.

Your actions are like a play on repeat,
But I have no interest in taking a seat.
I probably not would care if you do,
So keep on doing what you do.

With your empty words and fake smiles,
I see through your foolish guiles.
You think you can fool me with your act,
But I see the truth, that's a fact.

So go ahead and continue your charade,
I'll be laughing as the facade fades.
Do I care, probably not,
So keep on doing what you do, in this twisted plot.

WHY ARE YOU STILL TALKING?

Oh my god, why are you still talking?
Your words are like nails on a chalkboard screeching,
I'd rather listen to a cat constantly meowing,
Or a baby crying, soul-searching.

Your voice is like a never-ending nightmare,
Endless babbling, what a frightful sight,
Please stop talking, do us all a favor,
We're all suffering from your verbal blight.

Each word you speak is like a poison dart,
Injecting venom into our ears,
Oh my god, can't you see you're tearing us apart,
With your never-ending verbal cheers.

So please, for the love of all that's holy,
Give us all some peace and quiet,
Stop your incessant chatter, be jolly,
Oh my god, why are you still talking, it's a riot.

You're still reading this ~~shit~~?

That's embarrassing...

... good thing I don't care!

I DON'T HAVE WORDS FOR THIS ONE

In a world full of wit and charm,
Your stupidity sets off an alarm.
I don't have the words to explain,
The depth of your brain's disdain.

With each misguided thought you share,
I wonder if you're beyond repair.
My sarcasm might cut you deep,
But it's the only way to keep.

Your ignorance at bay,
And maybe, just maybe,
One day you'll see the light,
And finally get things right.

But until then, I'll just shake my head,
At the ridiculous things you've said.
I don't have words for your stupidity,
But my sarcasm might make you cry with hilarity.

SORRY, NOT SORRY!

In a world where rules bind tight,
I choose to live with all my might.
Sarcasm drips from every word,
Making some cry, how absurd!

I don't care for guidelines set,
I'll say what I please, no regret.
My humor sharp, my words like steel,
Beware, for my wit can make you feel.

So laugh along or run and hide,
My sarcasm is my joy, my pride.
I'll break the rules, make you cry,
But don't worry, it's all in good fun, oh why!

JOKES ASIDE

Excuse my sarcasm, it was meant for you
I thought you'd appreciate a joke or two
But I guess your sense of humor is lacking
In fact, it's downright attacking

I'll try to tone it down, be more sincere
But it's so hard when you're standing here
With that scowl upon your face
I'd rather be in outer space

So here's to you, my dear friend
May your frown never end
I'll keep my sarcasm to myself
And leave you in your pit of self

But just remember, I meant it for you
A little joke, a little skew
And if you ever want to laugh
Just give me a call, I'll be your telegraph.

THESE POEMS ARE GETTING SERIOUS

In the name of all that's holy,
Please cease your crazy ways,
My sarcasm is itching to escape
But I'll keep quiet, come what may.

Your antics never fail to amuse
But sometimes it's just too much,
I bite my tongue, hold back the snark
And plaster on a smile as such.

For the love of all that's good and right,
Just rein it in a bit,
My patience is wearing thin, my friend
But I won't throw a fit.

So please, for the love of God
Stop before I lose my cool,
I'll keep the sarcasm at bay
And try to keep my cool.

THIS ONE COULD MAKE YOU CRY

Oh, how I long to let my sarcasm run free,
But I keep my mouth shut for the love of thee,
Your behavior is like a never-ending show,
But I bite my tongue, not letting the sarcasm flow.

For the love of god, please stop your foolish ways,
I could roast you for hours, for days and days,
But instead, I'll hold back and keep the peace,
Even though your antics never seem to cease.

So here I am, biting my tongue in defeat,
Hoping that one day, you'll take a seat,
And realize the error of your foolish game,
Until then, I'll keep my sarcasm tame.

I DON'T HAVE A FILTER

In your presence, my sarcasm runs wild
No filter in sight, I'm like an unruly child
Your mere existence brings out the snark
Can't help but make a sarcastic remark

With every word you say, my wit does flow
Sarcasm is my way of letting you know
That your presence can be a bit much to bear
But hey, at least I've got a good sense of humor to spare

So here's to our banter, full of wit and jest
Who needs a filter when sarcasm is the best
In your company, I'll always be free
To let my true self shine, sarcastic as can be.

WHY SHOULD I BE KIND?

Oh why should I be kind, you ask with such disdain,
When your brain seems to be on an eternal holiday?
I'll ponder this question, though it may seem quite
inane,
Perhaps it's just my natural charm that leads the way.

For though your thoughts may wander like a lost sheep,
And your logic takes a vacation without a trace,
I'll still extend my kindness, not for your sake but to
keep,
Some shred of decency in this chaotic place.

So fear not, my dear friend with the broken brain,
I'll sprinkle some kindness on your path of confusion,
For in this world of madness and disdain,
A little bit of grace can lead to a peaceful conclusion.

You really made it this far?

What is wrong with you?

DID I HIT A NERVE, OOPS!

Oh, don't you fret about your woes,
For my sarcasm can handle those,
It'll gobble up your troubles, you'll see,
Leaving you in tears of glee.

I'll mock your worries with a grin,
Turning your frown into a silly grin,
My wit will slice through all your fears,
Leaving you laughing through your tears.

So go ahead, lay them at my feet,
Your problems and woes, I'll defeat,
With a quip and a jest, I'll make you see,
That laughter truly is the best remedy.

THESE POEMS COULD SET YOU FREE!

In a realm of wit and jest,
I'll mock your problems with my best.
Don't give a crap, I say with glee,
My sarcasm will set you free.

I'll make you laugh until you cry,
As I devour your troubles with a sly,
Grin upon my face, oh so smug,
Your woes will disappear in a tug.

So don't fret, my dear friend,
For I'll mock your problems until the end.
Just sit back, relax, and let me,
Turn your tears into laughter, you'll see.

I'M SARCASM ABOUT TO EXPLODE

My sarcasm's bubbling up, can't hold it in,
Because of you, my patience wearing thin.
Your cluelessness astounds me, don't you see?
My wit's about to explode, oh dear me!

I try to be polite, give you a chance,
But you keep on with your ignorance dance.
You're like a bull in a china shop, so blind,
And my sarcasm's roaring, no longer confined.

I can't help but roll my eyes at your ways,
You're like a broken record on replay.
But oh, what fun it is to watch you squirm,
As my sarcasm burns with an fiery burn.

So keep it up, my dear oblivious friend,
For my sarcasm knows no bounds, no end.
And soon enough, you'll finally catch on,
To the humor in my words, so dry and drawn.

ALL BECAUSE OF YOU...

Oh dear, my sarcasm's primed to ignite
All because of you, what a delight
Your words are like a ticking time bomb
Ready to explode, causing quite the storm

Your obliviousness, it knows no bounds
My patience dwindles, it truly astounds
I'll keep my cool, or at least try to
But beware, my sarcasm's about to breakthrough

So keep your wits about you, my friend
Before my sharp tongue brings this to an end
For my sarcasm is a force to be reckoned
And with you around, it's surely beckoned

But fear not, it's all in good fun
Just a little game we like to shun
So let's embrace the wit and banter
And laugh together, in our little banter.

PLEASE...

My sarcasm is ready to burst at the seams,
All because of you and your silly schemes.
I try to be nice, I try to be kind,
But your ignorance leaves me way behind.

You think you're so clever, so wise and so cool,
But in reality, you're just a fool.
My words drip with sarcasm, sharp as a knife,
But it seems you can't grasp the humor in life.

So here I stand, on the verge of explosion,
Hoping you'll finally get the notion.
That sarcasm is my weapon, my shield in this war,
And I'll use it against you, forever more.

JUST STOP!

Oh dear, please just stop your foolish ways,
I can't bear another moment of your craze.
Your ignorance knows no bounds,
I feel like I'm surrounded by clowns.

I'll unleash my sarcasm, sharp and biting,
To show you just how wrong you are, so enlighting.
Your stupidity is truly astounding,
I'm amazed you haven't drowned in your own
confounding.

So listen up, and listen well,
Your brain must be as empty as a shell.
I'll mock you with every ounce of wit,
Until you finally realize that you're full of... nonsense.

UNTITLED

Oh please just stop, I can't bear anymore
Your stupidity seeps through every pore
I'll unleash my sarcasm, a tyrant you'll see
For your ignorance is just too much for me

You prattle on, with no sense in sight
I cringe at every word you recite
My eyes roll back, my patience wearing thin
I'll hit you with sarcasm, let the fun begin

Your foolishness knows no bounds
It's like listening to a pack of clowns
But fear not, for I'll match your folly
With sarcasm sharp and oh so jolly

So next time you speak, think twice my dear
For my sarcasm is always near
I'll mock you with wit, make you see
The error of your ways, with glee.

How can you
read this ~~shit~~?

Quite frankly...

... I don't care!

ODE TO ME

Oh how great is it to be me,
No filter, wild and free,
Sorry if my words spark your rage,
But hey, at least I'm all the rage.

I speak my mind, no holding back,
Sometimes it's a bit out of whack,
But why hide behind a mask,
When you can bask in my blunt sass.

So here's to me, unfiltered and true,
Sorry if it makes you turn blue,
Just remember, it's all in good fun,
Life's too short to be anyone but number one.

I. HATE. PEOPLE

I hate people, oh yes I do,
They lie and cheat, oh boo hoo.
With fake smiles and words untrue,
I'd rather be alone, wouldn't you?

They gossip and backstab, so sly,
While pretending to be a good guy.
But behind their masks, they lie,
Oh, how I wish they would just fly.

I'd rather be in the company of trees,
Their silence is much more pleasing to me.
No drama, no games, just gentle breeze,
Oh, the peace and tranquility I seize.

So let them chatter and continue their show,
I'll be here, happily on my own.
Away from the chaos, the fake glow,
In solitude, my heart can truly grow.

NOT FEELING IT

In this world so full of greed,
People's actions make my heart bleed,
Their selfish ways, oh how they shine,
I hate them all, they're not so fine.

They talk of love but only lie,
With twisted tongues and closed minds, oh why?
They take and take, but never give,
I hate them all, I hate to live.

Their fake smiles and empty words,
Their shallow hearts, like dirty birds,
I see right through their deceitful game,
I hate them all, they're all the same.

So let them pass, let them go,
I'll keep my distance, let them know,
I hate people, oh yes I do,
But I'll stay true, to myself, me, and you.

WHY THE STUPID QUESTIONS

Why do you ask such stupid questions,
Sarcasm is my pun,
I'll answer with witty suggestions,
And have myself some fun.

You don't seem to understand,
Or maybe you just don't care,
But I'll keep up my sarcastic brand,
And give you a mocking stare.

So keep on with your queries,
I'll keep on with my wit,
For sarcasm is my theories,
And I won't quit.

CAN'T STAND YOUR STUPIDITY

In a world full of wonder and joy,
You ask such stupid questions, oh boy.
Sarcasm is my pun, my witty retort,
For your inquiries, I must abort.

Why do you question the things I say?
Do you doubt my intelligence in some way?
My answers are sharp, my tone is dry,
I'll mock your queries till the day I die.

So keep on asking your foolish queries,
And I'll respond with sarcasm, never weary.
For in this game of wit and pun,
I'll always have the last laugh, my dear one.

YES I WENT THERE

Oh, how I love when you come near,
With your words that fill me with fear,
I'm not always sarcastic, oh no,
Just when you come along, you know.

You bring out the snark in me,
With every comment that you decree,
I can't help but roll my eyes,
At your never-ending supply of lies.

Oh, how I love our little chats,
Where I pretend to care about your stats,
I'm not always sarcastic, oh no,
Just when you come along, you so-and-so.

But deep down, beneath my wit,
There's a part of me that wants to quit,
I wish I could be more sincere,
But with you around, that's just not in here.

So here I'll stay, with my quips and jabs,
As you continue on with your verbal stabs,
I'm not always sarcastic, oh no,
Just when you come along, you silly so-and-so.

NO ITS JUST YOU

I'm not always sarcastic, oh no, just when you come
along
Your presence brings out the best in me, can't you tell
I'm having fun?
I'll mock your every move, your words, your silly little
song
But deep down, I'm just a clown, playing with my puns

You think I'm being mean, but really, I just can't resist
Your ignorance and arrogance, they make for quite the
twist
I'll poke and prod and jest, until you're feeling so
dismissed
But underneath it all, it's just a game of wit and bliss

So don't take me too seriously, I'm just a joker in the
pack
I'll laugh and tease and mock, but it's all just a playful
act
I'm not always sarcastic, oh no, just when you come
along
So take a joke, have some fun, and play along with my
song.

PRETTY SURE ITS YOU NOT ME

Oh, aren't you just a gem,
You must be the problem, I contend,
That's why I'm so mean,
With my sarcasm, I offend.

Your presence brings out the worst,
In my biting wit and sly remarks,
But don't worry, I'm well-versed,
In using sarcasm as my dark arts.

So thank you for being the catalyst,
For my sharp tongue and dry humor,
I'll continue to be acridist,
Until you learn to be a bit more self-assured.

But until then, I'll just keep on flinging,
My sarcastic barbs at you,
Because it's clear you're the one clinging,
To the role of being the clueless fool.

Can't believe your still here, if you made it this far...

... you must seriously have problems.

how do I feel about that?

read chapter 6 page 19, ohhh wait!

ANOTHER UNTITLED: PROBLEM?

In the land of sarcasm, I reign supreme
With words sharp as a razor, cutting your self-esteem
You're pretty sure I'm the problem, causing your
distress
But darling, your cluelessness is truly a mess

I'm just a mirror reflecting your flaws
But instead of facing them, you blame me for your cause
So keep on believing I'm the reason you're mean
While I'll bask in the glory of my sarcasm's sheen

You may not like the truth that my words unveil
But darling, it's not me, it's your ego that fails
So go ahead and point fingers, play the victim's game
I'll just sit back and laugh at your misplaced blame

For in the world of sarcasm, I'll always be queen
And you'll forever be the target of my sharp-witted
scene
So keep on believing I'm the problem to your dismay
But deep down inside, you know you're the one to
betray.

THINGS I CAN'T SAY: PART 1

In company I keep my mouth shut tight,
For fear of stirring up a fight,
I bite my tongue and smile politely,
Even though my thoughts are unsightly.

There are things I want to say,
But I know they'll just cause dismay,
So I keep them locked away,
And pretend everything's okay.

It's foolishness that keeps me quiet,
I want to scream and start a riot,
But instead I'll nod and agree,
And let stupidity run free.

So here I am, a silent fool,
Playing by society's rule,
But deep inside, I cannot deny,
The things I can't say, but want to cry.

THINGS I CAN'T SAY: PART 2

There are things I dare not speak,
For fear of appearing meek,
But oh, the stupidity I see,
Makes me want to scream with glee.

The ignorance and foolish ways,
Leave me in a daze,
Oh, how I long to make them see,
But alas, it's not meant to be.

So I bite my tongue and hold my peace,
And watch as they wander in mental cease,
But deep inside, I want to shout,
Wake up, you fools, figure it out!

But alas, I must stay quiet,
Suppress my urge to incite,
For some things are better left unsaid,
Even if it fills me with dread.

THINGS I CAN'T SAY: PART ~~890~~ 3

In the land of fools and dimwits, I dwell,
Where truth and reason bid farewell.
There are things I long to speak out loud,
But stupidity reigns, and I'm disallowed.

I want to shout, "You're a fool, can't you see?"
But biting my tongue is the better decree.
For logic and sense are lost on you,
In your world of ignorance, old and new.

I wish to say, "You're wrong, it's clear as day,"
But your thick skull blocks the truth's display.
So I'll keep my thoughts locked up tight,
In the realm of the dumb, where wrong is right.

Oh, the things I can't say to people, but want to say,
Because their stupidity rules the day.
But I'll keep my wit sharp and my tongue in check,
In this ballad of fools, a sarcastic ode to respect.

SOMTHING, I DARE UTTER NOT!

There are things I long to say
But hold my tongue each day
For fear of sounding dumb
And causing quite a humdrum

I want to tell them their ideas are silly
And their actions downright willy-nilly
But I bite my tongue with great restraint
To avoid their ignorant complaint

Oh the things I can't express
Because of their foolishness
I'll keep them locked inside
And let my sarcasm hide

For speaking up would be a waste
On minds that can't keep pace
So I'll keep my thoughts at bay
And nod along in dismay

AGH, I HATE PEOPLE: ~~STUPIDITY!~~

In this world full of fools, oh how I despise
Their ignorance and arrogance, it truly belies
I bite my tongue to keep from looking dumb
For speaking my mind will only leave me glum

They prattle on with empty words and thoughts
Their brains like empty vessels, tied up in knots
I shake my head in disbelief at their folly
Oh, how I long to escape from this melancholy

But alas, I am stuck in this world so absurd
Where stupidity reigns, it's truly absurd
So I'll keep my sarcasm sharp and at bay
And silently mock them as they go on their way.

I'M NOT EVEN HALF WAY DONE

Oh, how I adore humanity,
So wise and full of grace,
Their brilliance shines so brightly,
I'm in awe of every face.

Their words are like sweet melodies,
Their thoughts, so deep and grand,
I bask in their intelligence,
And marvel at their command.

But wait, what's this I see?
A cloud upon my view,
People can be quite foolish,
And oh, so dim, it's true.

I hate the way they stumble,
And fall in their own trap,
If I were to speak my mind,
I'd surely look like a sap.

So here I sit, in wonder,
At the brilliance all around,
I love people, oh so dearly,
Sarcasm so profound.

I'm not even done, why did I choose 100 pages... god!

these poems
are so stupid!

if your reading this, for the love of god, do something else!

A BLANK POEM BECAUSE I JUST CAN'T THINK OF PUNS!

--blank poem--

ODE TO MY WORKPLACE!

Oh work place, how I despise thee,
My co-workers are fine, but my manager, oh she's a bee
Her words drip with negativity,
Making each day a dreadful reality

With her constant criticism and disdain,
I feel like I'm going insane
I try to smile and play nice,
But her toxic presence is like ice

Oh work place, you're a place of dread,
With my manager filling me with dread
But I'll soldier on, with a smile on my face,
Because in this ballad, sarcasm takes its place.

ODE TO MY SIBLINGS!

In the house where we dwell,
My siblings cause me hell,
With their antics and their pranks,
Sometimes I want to give them thanks.

For all the joy they bring,
With their constant nagging,
I can't help but want to scream,
And maybe give a little kick or beam.

But beneath it all, I know,
Their love for me does show,
So I'll put up with their teasing,
And cherish these moments, pleasing.

For in the end, they are family,
And their quirks make me happy,
So here's to my siblings, dear,
For always being near.

THIS POEM IS ALL OVER THE PLACE!

Oh, this poem's a real masterpiece,
So scattered it's hard to find some peace,
I stopped caring, what a relief,
The words just roll off like a thief.

From here to there, all over the place,
No rhythm or rhyme, just a disgrace,
But who cares, no need to impress,
Just throw it all out, what a mess.

I used to worry about each line,
But now I see it's all just fine,
Let chaos reign, let words run free,
This poem's a reflection of me.

So here it is, a ballad so grand,
Full of sarcasm, unplanned,
I've stopped caring, let it be known,
This scattered poem is all my own.

I STOPPED CARING ABOUT YOU...

I stopped caring about you, toxic little thing,
Your drama and chaos, it's just not my fling,
You bring nothing but trouble, trouble and strife,
I'd rather be alone than deal with your life.

You're like a poison, seeping into my day,
I'll pass on the drama, I'm better off this way,
I won't cry a river or mourn our lost bond,
I'll just sit back and watch as you carry on.

So toxic and draining, you've lost all my care,
I'll find peace and happiness elsewhere,
Good luck with your drama, your problems, your mess,
I'll be over here, living my best.

EVENTUALLY THESE POEMS WILL END: THEY SUCK!

Oh, my dear, your words cut deep
Making me want to release my sarcasm in a heap
My poems may suck, that much is true
But it's all thanks to the anger you brew

Each line dripping with venom and spite
Turning my words into a poetic fight
But I'll keep writing, no matter how bad
For your anger only makes me more glad

So go on, fuel my fiery verse
My sarcasm will only get worse
And though my poems may not be grand
They're a reflection of your bitter demand

So keep on pushing, keep on being mad
For with each word, I'm not all that sad
Your anger, my muse, in poetry's delight
Creating verses that pack a sarcastic bite.

I WANT TO HIT SOMEONE SO BAD

In my mind, I want to throw a punch,
Let my anger out in a crunch.
But instead, I bite my tongue,
Keep my sarcasm tightly strung.

I won't stoop to their level,
No need for a physical revel.
I'll keep my wit sharp as a knife,
Cut them down without the strife.

So when you see me smile and nod,
Know that beneath the facade,
There lies a simmering rage,
Locked away in a cage.

I'll let my words do the fighting,
Put them in their place, igniting.
No need for violence, just a jest,
To leave them feeling less than best.

YUP, I WENT THERE: BURN BABY!

In my mind, I stew and seethe,
Wanting to lash out and let it heave,
But I bite my tongue, hold back the rage,
Keeping my sarcasm in its cage.

I want to hit someone so bad,
But I'll keep my cool and not go mad,
For violence solves nothing, they say,
So I'll just keep my thoughts at bay.

I'll swallow my words, bite my lip,
And keep my composure, just a quip,
Sarcasm my shield, my saving grace,
Keeping me from crossing that dangerous space.

So I'll smile and nod, pretend it's fine,
While inside, I seethe and pine,
But better to keep quiet, keep the peace,
And let my sarcasm be my release.

I'm almost ~~f*cking~~ done.

I can't even
think of
anymore
poetry!

THINGS I SHOULDN'T SAY: PART 1

Oh dear, my sarcasm knows no bounds,
I should keep quiet, but it always resounds.
I can't help but let slip a snarky remark,
Even though I know it may cause a spark.

I jest and I jibe, with a smug little grin,
Knowing full well the trouble I'm in.
I shouldn't say these things to people, it's true,
But my sarcasm just comes bursting through.

I try to keep it in check, but it's a losing fight,
My words cut like a knife, sharp and tight.
So if you find yourself on the receiving end,
Just know it's all in jest, my sarcastic friend.

THINGS I SHOULDN'T SAY: PART 2

In courtly jest, my words do stray,
To mock and tease in merry way,
But oft they veer to cruel array,
And pierce like blades of cold dismay.

I jest and jibe, my tongue so sharp,
With sarcasm's bite, I play my part,
Yet careless whispers tear apart,
The fragile bonds of friends now smart.

I laugh and scoff, my wit so sly,
To mask the hurt that lies nearby,
But truth betrays the clever lie,
And friendships fade like evening sky.

So heed my warning, friend so dear,
Beware the words that sting and sear,
For sarcasm's blade, though deft and clear,
Can wound the heart and bring a tear.

I'M DONE OKAY, JEEZ!

In the realm of stupid poems I've toiled,
For you, my patience nearly spoiled.
Your actions, they do anger me so,
Sarcasm is the only way to go.

I'm almost done with this charade,
Writing for you feels like a crusade.
My words dripping with cynicism,
My frustration, a silent criticism.

These missives penned with ire and spite,
Each line a venomous poetic bite.
I'll finish these poems with a sneer,
For your insensitivity, my dear.

ALMOST DONE, MY GOD!

In a ballad I shall sing
Of the poems I used to bring
But now I'm almost done
With this game that you've won

Your actions piss me off
And sarcasm starts to scoff
These stupid poems I wrote
Are now sinking like a boat

But fear not, my dear friend
For this is not the end
I'll bid you adieu with grace
And let sarcasm take its place

So here's to you, my muse
For giving me the blues
I hope you find some joy
In knowing you've annoyed

But now I'm almost done
With these stupid poems, hon
So farewell, goodbye
I'll take my sarcasm and fly.

STOP NAGGING, YOU SOUND LIKE MY MOTHER!

Oh stop your whining, can't you see,
You sound just like my mother, dear me;
Always nagging, fussing, and prying,
My god, I feel like I'm slowly dying.

You pick and poke at every little thing,
As if I'm a puppet on a string;
Your voice like a song that never ends,
My patience wearing thin, it all depends.

I know you mean well, I truly do,
But can't you see, I need some space too;
Let me breathe, let me roam,
Before I turn into a grumpy gnome.

So please, my dear, spare me the drama,
I promise I won't cause any more trauma;
Just let me be, let me fly,
And maybe then, I won't have to sigh.

I can't believe you stayed to the end of this book...

I'm ~~f*cking~~ done, my sarcasm was wasted on you!

I hope you didn't enjoy this book!

I wanted to have
"books by author"
here...

.... you can go to Amazon and
find them, your a big boy/girl!

I wanted to put an "about author" section here...

A Note on the Author

Dina Ezzeddine is a writer and illustrator from Canada. Dina has a degree in Visual Arts and Design, as well as a Bachelor of Arts degree in English. Dina has written numerous children's book and numerous teen books. This book of poetry is her latest work. You can find more of Dina's upcoming work online!

----

author_illustratordina

aiko10195@gmail.com

missDinaAuthor

LEAVE US A REVIEW!

(honestly, I don't care if you do)

⭐⭐⭐⭐⭐

... but I don't care enough to do so!